TRANSFORMATIONAL

FULL BLOOM

JOURNEY OF GROWTH AND FULFILLMENT

LONDON HOWARD

Copyright © 2023 by London Howard
All rights reserved.

No part of this book may be used or reproduced in whole or in part, without written permission from the publisher, except by a reviewer, who may quote brief passages in a review; nor may any part of this book be reproduced, stored in a retrieval system, or transmitted in any form or by any means, electronic, mechanical, photocopying, recording, or other, without written permission from the publisher.

Printed in the United States of America
First printing, 2023
ISBN 979-8-218-30837-7
www.conversationwithlondon.com
www.londonhowardphotography.com
Book cover photo by Adina Howard

I DEDICATE THIS BOOK TO MY AMAZING PARENTS,

WITHOUT YOU, THERE IS NO ME.

LHW

Contents

Introduction	VII
1. PLANTING SEEDS OF CHANGE	1
2. SEEDLING MANUAL	13
3. NURTURING THE LEAP	23
4. SOWING FINANCIAL SEEDS	29
5. CULTIVATING SELF LOVE	35
6. BLOOM IN VULNERABILITY	41
7. UPROOTING FEAR	47
8. GROWING IN SUPPORTIVE SOIL	53
9. FERTILIZING POSITIVITY	61
10. JUST BE PATIENT	71
11. I WANT MY FLOWERS	75
Journal	79

Acknowledgement	91
References	92
Social Media	93

Introduction

Full Bloom – A 90-day Transformational Journey of Growth and Fulfillment, is a personal account of my *LEAP* from corporate America into the entrepreneurial world in photography. Breaking through the glass ceiling, and leaving on my terms, I finally liberated myself from the confines of my limiting beliefs. Each chapter reveals experiences that expose moments of self-doubt, determination and the audacity to bet on myself as I seek to discover my calling.

As you join me on my journey, we'll rewind the clock to my early days as an enthusiastic student in photography, and witness my evolution into a risk-taker. Within these pages you'll read about self-accountability, resilience, resources , faith and the strength I found along the way.

On this journey, you'll also have opportunities for some soul-searching introspection of your own. Let, ***Full Bloom*** be your *next level* guide, so get ready to shift your perspective and cultivate your personal blooming season.

Chapter One

PLANTING SEEDS OF CHANGE

Have you ever wished for a Monday to miraculously transform into a Friday, just as you're walking through the doors of your workplace? It never fails to amuse me because, in my memories, I can recall countless occasions throughout my careers, when the temptation to do a Sha'Carri Richardson sprint back to my vehicle, and drive straight home. Needless to say, due to my moral compass and work ethic, I would never allow myself to be that irresponsible and jeopardize a good job, as my mother would have cautioned. Growing up as part of GenX, I believe we embraced personal accountability, and are also unwilling to gamble our hard-earned future retirement or pension contributions for a fleeting moment of carelessness that will pass by lunchtime.

It's pretty amazing how the years can just sneak by so fast, often without even realizing it. What started as a five-year commitment with my former employer somehow transformed into a full-blown decade. Please don't get me wrong; it wasn't all bad. In fact, I had some incredible experiences during my time there. However, during this period, I found myself pulled in two different directions. On one hand, I had the responsibility of managing the day-to-day, tasks of my photography business, which I lovingly call my passion work. On the other hand, I had to put on my corporate hat and be effective and efficient at the brokerage firm. Juggling these distinct career paths was my way of trying to strike a work-life balance. Yet, despite my best efforts, I couldn't shake the nagging feeling of incompleteness.

In my position I had the responsibility of having to work with financial advisors', whom on many occasions a hand full just called to yell, complain, belittle, or just failed to take accountability for their lack of action. Now, grant it, there were some justified pain-points, but these interactions created a work environment that wasn't just unhealthy, but downright toxic! When you're in it, you don't realize how your body is being affected, both mentally and physically. This kind of workplace forces you to ask yourself: is the money really worth it?

When the stresses of my workday were too much to bear, I knew that I needed a mental break. I took full advantage of my evening and weekend, to focus my attention to on my photography business being a youth sports photographer. It was like a prescription from a doctor, just being able to step away from bad behaving adults acting like children.

Immersing myself in my passion work, was the perfect remedy to recenter and rejuvenate myself. It's genuinely astonishing how shifting your perspective for just an hour or two, can redirect your body's energy in an entirely different direction. Capturing moments like a 3-year-old attempting to balance on a soccer ball with their little foot, or a 10-year-old dribbling a basketball down the court, aiming for the bleachers instead of their teammate, was truly priceless. Allowing my shutter to fly, freezing these moments of happiness in an instant, became my solace.

I found it a necessity to find multiple best practices to decompress from the stresses of my work day, and clear my head. Take a look at my list below, and if you find yourself in a similar stressful situation try to incorporate one of these best practice for yourself. As you begin to take your first steps toward change, remember you have to take care of your mind and your body.

5 BEST PRACTICES – STRESS RELIEF

1. **Exercise Regularly**: Incorporating physical activity into your routine release's endorphins, which naturally changes one's mood. Even a short walk,

yoga session, or quick workout can help reduce stress. Consider joining a gym or walking around your neighborhood.

2. **<u>Practice Gratitude</u>**: Journaling or taking time to reflect on the day's events is a great stress reliever. Practicing gratitude by writing what you are thankful for, allows you to focus on positive aspects of your life and can shift your perspective.

3. **<u>Maintain a Healthy Diet</u>**: You are what you eat is the saying, and having a balanced diet by incorporating more fruits, vegetables, and whole grains is what the doctor orders. I found myself consuming more coffee and sugar, when I had my corporate hat on, which only contributed to my stress and anxiety. It's so essential to take care of our bodies, since we only have one life to live.

4. **<u>Establish Boundaries</u>**: It important to set clear boundaries between work and personal life, but it's just as important to keep them. One way to accomplish this is leave the laptop off when you are outside of work hours to prevent burnout and maintain a sense of balance.

5. **<u>Connect with Supportive People</u>**: Have a support system! It's so easy for me to retreat in the comforts of

> my home and lock the door. But what good would that be when I have amazing family members and friends who are willing to provide emotional support. It so important to share your feelings and experiences with others, because it can be a powerful way to relieve stress and gain new perspective.

I came to the realization that my tenure in the corporate world was limited, when I began to meticulously started counting down to the 86,400 seconds within each 24-hour day. Shockingly, 30,600 of those seconds were dedicated to the pursuit of someone else's dream. This persistent awareness that my time wasn't authentically mine weighed heavily on me, leaving me with an insatiable desire to reclaim it.

After the pandemic I seen firsthand how the workplace was no longer as desirable to retreat to. This was evident with the daily news reports that unemployment was on the rise, and people opting out to returning back to the office setting. I believe this was partially caused by people being forced to shift their focus from projects and deadlines, to family matters and finally shinning a light on their own level of happiness. I like many stuck it out with our employer, because the safety net of employment is a whole lot easier to lean into, rather than facing an unpredictable future and being unemployed.

During the transitioning period after the pandemic, I understood that this time was meant for me to find clarity;

create, learn, hone in on new skills, and above all make time to prioritize my own self-care. We will revisit self-love and self-care in the upcoming chapters.

As I listened to the inner voice within me, posing the question: *"When will that moment arrive?"* I found myself without a concrete answer. But the more I thought about it, the more I recognized the imperative need for a decision— one that had to come sooner rather than later.

The decision to initiate significant changes in my career came sooner than expected, and it was in many ways inevitable. This tipping point moment coincided with the new year going into 2023, when I found myself realigned to a different team within the brokerage firm. While this transition didn't catch me completely off guard, it did bring a shift in leadership and guidance, and a new set of rules, after having established a strong five-year rapport with my previous team leader.

It's often said that change can be *"bittersweet,"* and in this case, I attest to the truth of that sentiment. Leaving behind the comfort and familiarity of my former team wasn't an easy decision, but it wasn't mine to begin with. However, the prospect of joining a new team with a fresh perspective and a different dynamic was undeniably exciting.

Leadership always has its reasons for implementing change, and with that my own decision prompted a significant realization within me. If I was considered valuable enough to assist in the growth of another team, it became apparent that I should place an even higher value on my own photography company and fully commit to nurturing its growth. With this newfound clarity, the gears of my exit strategy started to turn.

I accepted that my 11-year journey with my employer was coming to an end, and I made the ultimate decision to begin drafting my resignation letter. This decision was not as straightforward as I had initially imagined. A wave of emotions swept over me, and self-doubt briefly crept in – starting all my questions with the w's "what, why, when, where". Nevertheless, I swiftly pushed those doubts aside, I was ready to close this chapter of my journey.

During this introspective process, I couldn't help but express my gratitude for the numerous life lessons and valuable experiences that this company provided over the years. I've had the privilege of wearing various hats, taking on roles as both a self and people leader. This journey had shed light on the importance of not always being the most vocal presence in the room, yet still making a significant impact. I took great pride in knowing the contributions I made over the years would continue to benefit both current and future employees for years to come.

Being part of this company has been a privilege, despite the inherent challenges that came with the seat I held. I deeply value the time I spent there, and this experience has indelibly shaped me, just as I have influenced the organization in return.

With the wheels of change now set in motion, and my sights firmly fixed on shaping my own unique path, I stood ready for the next chapter of my journey. If I envisioned the next five years differing from the last, it became my responsibility to plant the seeds of my new future now.

On the morning of March 27, 2023, I drew in a deep breath, and as I exhaled, I mustered the courage to press the send button on my email, officially submitting my two-week resignation letter.

Making this decision wasn't easy; it took me nearly four years to reach this point after wavering back and forth. I knew what I was asking of myself required me to have strength, consistency and most of all I had to put in the work with my faithful leap. The last question I posed to myself was, will my photography business withstand the test of time? When you feel that strong desire for something more, well I had that unshakeable sense come over me that my life had a higher purpose, and I had no choice but to act on it. I knew I needed a solid exit strategy, well at least as solid as possible.

My exit strategy evolved over the years, fluctuating between required my savings account, paying off debts, and handling unexpected expenses. When you're contemplating your next move, doing some extra legwork and confronting those tough questions can save you from unnecessary stress.

I've compiled a personal list of questions that guided me before I took the leap. Now, here's my question for you: What's on your list?

10 QUESTIONS – EXIT STRATEGY CONSIDERATION

1. **What was my ultimate long-term vision**? Take time to really sit down and ask yourself, what is my personal and professional goals beyond corporate life.

2. **Do I have enough money in savings to sustain my livelihood**? Ensure you have enough savings or investments to support your transition to entrepreneurship.

3. **What am I going to offer the world that is unique and of value**? Identify your talents, skills and expertise that will set you apart, and make you marketable in your industry.

4. **What does the current market look like for my business, do I have a plan B**? Research the demand for your skills in your desired industry or entrepreneurial venture.

5. **Continued or new health care**? No one wants to be without health care, and I recommend you consult the human resource department immediately. I found that COBRA has an adsorbent cost associated for me to afford, so I had to seek out other insurance companies. Again, do not wait until the last minute to confirm your policy terms.

6. **How much notice should I provide my employer**? I provided a two week notice when I resigned my position. I know some of you might say, well employers don't extend the same courtesy when they terminate employees. If this is your situation, you have to decide what works best for you.

7. **Am I ready for change**? It's important to prepare for change, and not act on pure emotions only. There will be uncertainties throughout your journey and of post corporate life.

8. **Have I built a personal brand**? I have been blessed to say yes, to this question. For seven years I have worked in sports photography and have been building and growing my clientele.

9. **What's my marketing and networking strategy**? Growth is essential for business to survive and thrive. Find a way to Develop a plan for promoting your skills

or business for existing and new potential clients or employers.

10. **Am I open to learning and adapting**? This question was easy to me to answer with a yes. Yes, I am open to learn new skills from other photographers or instructors. I learn something new about myself every day, and am not afraid to ask questions if I don't' have the answer.

Chapter Two

SEEDLING MANUAL

Friday, April 7, 2023, marked a truly Good Friday for me! As I hung up the phone on the final day of my corporate job, I knew my journey toward a fresh start had officially begun. I closed my eyes and leaned back in my office chair, and a wave of emotions washed over me. With my head resting against the chair, I closed my eyes as a trail of happy tears trickled down my cheek. I parted my lips slightly and whispered ever so softly, *"I did it!"*

With my eyes still shut, I begin to reminisce about how I had arrived at this moment. This leap had not come without its fair share of trial and error, extreme highs, and crashing lows in my photography journey.

Let me take you back to my disastrous first experience photographing a wedding for a childhood friend, more than 20 years ago, despite being cautioned by my sister against it in the first place. To grasp why it was a complete disaster, picture a medium-sized church with minimal natural light and a wedding party that could have doubled as a small family reunion. And then there was me— an enthusiastic, young photographer hired for $500.00 to document a childhood friend's wedding day.

I was armed with a Nikon N80— yes, film photography in a world before digital cameras, where you had to wait for film development to see the results. I had to master my settings, which wouldn't happen for another 20 years. I'd also need to adjust for changing conditions, and wait for film development. But let's not get too ahead of ourselves.

Before I traveled back to my hometown of Grand Rapids, I purchased what I thought was an amazing mounted flash. There is a saying by photographers *"Don't use new equipment for the first time on a big assignment, especially if you don't know how it works."* Can you see where this is headed?

In the days leading up to the wedding, I stayed up late reading the manual for my SB-50DX speedlight. If you're facepalming right now, I understand — I just did it myself. Now, let's fast forward to the wedding day. I started by capturing all the essential moments as the bride had requested. I mentally checked off each important shot as I went. The ceremony went smoothly, and I glided through it, capturing every detail— from the procession and ring exchange to the candle ceremony and broom jumping. And, of course, I didn't miss the all-important first kiss. I continued snapping away, capturing the entire wedding party in various poses.

As the evening wrapped up I captured imagery consisting of the first dance, garter toss, and the wedding party running down a hill, you might be thinking, "*This doesn't sound so bad.*"

However, the real twist came when I returned to Las Vegas, gathered up 15 rolls of film, and headed to Wolf Camera, a highly reputable camera store, to develop my film. After a couple of days, the prints were ready for me to review. I paid my outstanding $150 or so dollars for developing the film to the cashier, then eagerly opened the first envelope containing the prints. The photos of the bride getting ready were beautiful, and my smile widened. But as I continued to flip through, my smile quickly turned into a frown. I realized that the images taken inside the church were underexposed. Panic set in as I exclaimed, "*Oh no!*"

I asked the representative if this could be fixed, but I received a disappointing head shake and an apology "*I'm sorry, there's nothing we can do.*" Inside me, a piece of happiness withered away.

> How on earth was I going to explain this to my friend, also the bride? I believe that being honest and upfront was the best approach, as I felt it does allow for a quicker processing of the disappointment, rather than me prolonging the inevitable and stressing. So, I mustered the courage to make the phone call. I explained that some of the images were underexposed and that I would be sending the photo album for her to review. Let's just say that the review didn't go well, and a full refund was promptly sent back.

Luckily, my beginning story is not my final one, and I grew stronger and wiser over the years. I have clients for which I still have to ask myself *"what is the best approach to resolve this issue?"* Whenever you are directly involved with face-to-face interaction, I have to remind myself to be prepared for the unexpected.

As I opened my eyes, an overwhelming sense of gratitude washed over me, and I expressed my thanks to God once more for granting me the courage to move forward on this significant leap. This act of faith held profound significance in my life, as it marked the moment when I took control of my employment destiny. I was mentally prepared to enter a world that did not have glass ceilings, one where I could shatter any limiting beliefs and embrace the abundance that awaited, for I knew that the sky held no limits and I was ready to soar.

Before making this leap, I had a clear understanding of what I was leaving behind— the comfort of a stable paycheck. Now, I was venturing into a realm where my success relied solely on my own efforts, which demanded self-motivation. While I don't have all the answers, I was willing to take calculated risks by dedicating myself to photography and creating strategies to maximize my time and opportunities to generate multiple streams of income. After all, it's through taking risks that we reap the most significant rewards.

There exist numerous blueprints for success, but determining the right one can be a challenge. I went down my own checklist and reviewed it carefully, savings, a budding photography business, a fierce mindset tuned in for success, and good health. While reviewing my SMART goals, I reminded myself it also included my faith, which would not permit me to fail, no matter what the odds. I had to ask myself, "have I done enough to prepare, to ensure success on this leap?" and remembered my morning mantra.

"I DO ENOUGH, I HAVE ENOUGH, I AM ENOUGH"

Success was mine for the taking, and I was ready to find it. Without missing a beat, I plunged into action, the next day I focused my attention to returning my corporate equipment and required paperwork. It felt liberating, even though it took a week for them to receive it. I was still finally ready to release the old desk that had held me captive for too long. I was finally free to own my entire day without having to clock in.

My first goal was to reclaim my health and well-being. Focusing on the SMART method, I committed to reclaiming peace of mind and well-being by working out 3-4 days a week, getting sufficient sleep, and dedicating my morning for mindful meditative practices. I was able to outline each goal I set for myself, following up with refining my photography skills, and learning from both triumphs and setbacks. This next 90 days was my time of discovery, a period in which I was able to tap back into my creative side that had been dormant for too long, and identify my niche within the entrepreneurial world.

Here's how I incorporated the SMART goal method to regain my health and shed 30 pounds. Many of us share the same aspiration of losing weight, and I'm no exception. I'd like to share how I've utilized SMART goals to work towards reclaiming my health.

S.M.A.R.T. GOAL

S: <u>SPECIFIC</u>: Make your goal specific and narrow for more effective planning.

- I aim to walk a minimum of 10K steps 3-4 days every week.

M: <u>MEASURABLE</u>: Make sure your goal and progress are measurable.

- I will track my daily step count using a fitness tracker or smartphone app to ensure I consistently achieve this goal.

A: <u>ATTAINABLE</u>: Make sure you can reasonably accomplish your goal within a certain time frame.

- To make this goal attainable, I will start with 3 days a week and gradually work up to 4 days as my fitness level improves. In addition, I will consult with health care professional to ensure it aligns with my health needs.

R: <u>RELEVANT</u>: Your goal should align with your values and long-term objectives.

- Walking is a low impact exercise that is suitable for most fitness levels and supports weight loss and overall health improvement, aligning with my goal to lose 30 pounds ad reclaim my health.

T: TIME-BASED: Set a realistic but ambitious end date to clarify task prioritization and increase motivation.

- I will work towards this goal over the next eight months, with aim of losing 30 lbs. and significantly improving my overall health by December 31, 2023. I will regularly assess my progress and make necessary adjustments to ensure I stay on track.

Taking my leap had to have structure and direction, and like the old saying goes: "*If you don't plan, you plan to fail.*" For me I had to map this part of my journey out, if I wanted it to be a successful one. If you're anything like me planning is a must. Allow me to set you up for success. Use this worksheet to plan your next steps.

SCAN QR CODE – S.M.A.R.T. Goals worksheet

Chapter Three

NURTURING THE LEAP

It amazes me how little time I actually was working with after a *"long day"* at my corporate job. Now with all the newfound time in my day I was responsible to structure it as I saw fit. I basked briefly in the glow of my life's course at the start of my day. However, time was of the essence, and I didn't have time to waste. I felt as if I had so much to do, and the very first order of business was scheduling all of my doctor's appointments. You know, those annual visits that require you to relax, relate and breathe.

I found myself in a pickle because my previous employer's healthcare benefits terminated at midnight the day I resigned, and not at the end of the month. If you're saying "*wow*", I was too, because I was slightly thrown off-guard by this timeframe. I was under the impression I had until the end of the month, which was so far removed from the truth. So, I would be remiss if I didn't give you this advice, which is to make sure you familiarize yourself with all of your existing benefits prior to leaving your employer. Now, I'm not saying this should stop your forward movement, but you should be prepared for any surprises. If you have taken the following eight steps prior to making your final decision to leap and the fabric of your core is screaming: "I want you to take my hand," allow me to guide you as to what your next 90-day journey might look like.

7 STEPS TO TAKE PRIOR TO TAKING YOUR LEAP

1. **Mindset**: Is this rational? You don't want to be impulsive regarding your LEAP into the unknown without weighing the pros and cons.

2. **Meet with your team leader**: Are you wanting small changes or have you outgrown the company? If having a conversation with your leader is worth a try, share with them your prepared talking points. Make sure you understand what the meeting objectives are.

3. **More money**: This is your time to be direct. If you want more money, take time to share your desired

amount. This is your opportunity to read Never Split the Difference by Chris Voss. Use the art of negotiation. What do you have to lose if they say no?

4. **Relocating desk**: Have you ever wanted to work from home? If you answered yes, and your workplace extends this option, you may want to consider asking if being a virtual employee is an option. I was a virtual agent for the four years up to my leap. Working remotely has simultaneous benefits and challenges. But if you can stick it out this might be an option for you. I will go into more details regarding my experience in the upcoming chapters.

5. **Too blessed to stress**: There are various reasons to do a self-introspection and one is when you start telling yourself "*Enough is enough.*" If you have drilled down and identified the source of stress, whether it is a hostile work environment, lack of pay, long commute, or micromanaging, it might be time to explore other options. What is your WHY?

6. **Create a financially prepared leap**: Are you financially prepared? Financial advisors have expressed having six-month savings, but from my experience, I would suggest you shoot for one year if possible. There might be unexpected expenses that will arise, and when

they do, you want to be prepared. *"A Consumer Affairs 2021 study, held in the aftermath of the pandemic, found 42% of those who left their jobs in 2021, say they were financially prepared. 60% who left said they came out ahead financially."* The three key financial preparations before quitting were: (1)Setting aside savings for monthly expenses (2) Creating a monthly budgeT (3) Reducing nonessential spending. If you can stick to these key factors, you have a receipt for success.

7. **<u>Cut the toxic cords</u>**: Taking care of yourself physically, spiritually and mentally cannot be emphasized enough. Did you know that the number one day out of the week with increased rates of heart attacks is Monday? Sometimes, you might not realize your environment could be costing you your health and wellbeing until you are able to step away, and look at the big picture with a fresh pair of lenses. We are living in a world where we are taking days off for mental health is the norm. During my last year, I found myself taking more days off due to being mentally exhausted from the demands of previous day; not having the strength to walk across my living room floors to log in. Many workplaces offer psychologists due to the heightened public awareness around this matter. For me, the toxicity cord had to be severed, and

once I did that, I better understood my WHY!

As you can see, there are a number of steps you can consider prior to taking your own leap. If you are able to transition into self-employment smoothly, the process will be effortless. A smooth exit and transition into self-employment were my top priority. If I can help you out on your journey, take time to use these 7 steps for you to be better equip for your next chapter.

Chapter Four

SOWING FINANCIAL SEEDS

How do you plan to cover your monthly expenses? Do you have sufficient funds to support your current lifestyle? What financial preparation have you made? The financial questions will continue to come from various sources, so I'm here to address the million-dollar question. My answer is, *"If you're not willing to risk what you never had, you'll continue to receive what you've always gotten."*

Over the past 11 years working in corporate America, I've managed to create a solid nest egg specifically for my next chapter. I understand that many of you reading this may not find yourselves in the same financial situation, but if you share the same desire and determination to succeed, then I want you to come along with me on this journey.

During my first 90-days, financially, things were quite smooth because I hadn't had the need to tap into my savings at this point. I made it a priority to budget for my existing commitments and cut down on unnecessary spending, like dining out. One tool I find really reliable for managing my expenses and forecasting future expenses is QuickBooks.

This app completely changed the game for me, eliminating the hours I used to waste on Excel spreadsheets, hoping they would magically balance themselves in the end. If you're still stuck in the old-fashioned way of handling finances, it's time to say goodbye to the dinosaur age thinking and accept this more efficient accounting method to take control of the fight of your financial expenses.

Transitioning full-time to my entrepreneurial desk was an unnerving step for me. Leaving behind the safety net of my corporate desk, which I had depended on for years, was quite nerve wracking to say the least. Taking charge of my photography business required me becoming proficient in sales, a role I didn't actually identify with. I prefer to see myself as a passionate individual, trusting in my natural, God-given photographic talent, and, as my slogan says *"Bringing life's treasures into focus."* The prospect of relying solely on my efforts to generate monthly income, supporting both my personal and professional life, left me feeling unsettled. I needed to shift my mindset, and I needed to do it fast. Without the corporate desk to lean on, I had to learn to believe in myself.

I had to make peace with this mindset to step onto the somewhat lonely path all by myself. On April 7th, Good Friday, as I logged off the phone for the last time, no one could assure me that my journey wouldn't be riddled with doubts, fears, tears and days of isolation. The weight of negative financial emotions can be overwhelming, but with God by my side and the comforting reminder *"No weapon formed against you shall prosper" (Isaiah 54:17)* I had unwavering faith that I would persevere through any trials and tribulations that may come my way.

I urge you to embrace the spirit of a warrior, putting on the full armor of God for protection. When those doubts and thoughts of an inadequacy try to sneak into your journey, raise your invisible sword and declare *"NOT TODAY"* and keep pushing forward.

The subject of money can stir up a whirlwind of emotions, and there's a common misconception that having an overflowing bank account equates to ultimate happiness in life. I personally believe this to be far from the truth. It's only when you've lived long enough, experienced both wealth and had to rebuild from scratch that your perception on money may shift. You truly understand the value of money, or the lack thereof, when you no longer possess it or when it slips through your fingers.

However, money does grant you certain freedoms that may make the journey of life more manageable. My aspiration is to establish multiple streams of income, not just for my own present, but to create a lasting legacy for my family. I'm driven by the desire to pave the way for the next generation, including my niblings and their descendants. The progress I've made in my first 90-days, fueled by a purposeful beginning, continues to inspire me as I envision my future.

Financial literacy is extremely important to me, since I've had the pleasure of working for 11 years in the financial industry. During this time, I've had the privilege to be in an environment surrounded by knowledgeable leaders and financial advisors, conversing in passing with them on a daily basis.

In these discussions, planning for financial futures were their top priority and took center stage, leading me to question the age-old saying: *"If you don't plan for your future, you plan to fail."* I firmly believe in your potential for success, but I also recognize that without addressing financial challenges today, your journey may become more complex down the road.

To assist you on this journey, I invite you to ask yourself the following four. By reflecting on these questions, you can pave the way for a more secure and prosperous financial future.

What does your landscape look like in the next 6 months? How will you work towards financial stability during this time?

- **1 Year Ahead**: Looking one year into the future, what specific financial goals do you hope to have achieved? How will your expertise and financial resources have evolved?

- **Next 5 Years**: Over the next five years, what are your aspirations for your financial situation? Do you plan to diversify investments, enhance security, or explore new opportunities?

- **Financial Freedom**: What does financial freedom mean to you, and what steps are you taking to reach this state? Can you outline a tentative timeline for when you aim to achieve it, even if it's a dynamic goal?

SCAN QR CODE – Financial Landscape

Chapter Five

CULTIVATING SELF LOVE

Reflecting on the first 90 days, I have to describe it as if I was finally meeting my soulmate for the very first time. The initial connection was a warm embrace, the newness of a relationship that has you smiling in the morning from ear to ear. There was an undeniable ease to the familiarity, as if time and I had formed a special bond prior to our encounter, one that allowed me to glide through each day with grace and purpose.

As the sun settled into the distance, and the world rested into the quiet of the night, I found solace in the stillness. While tucking myself in, my thoughts would drift towards the endless possibilities that lay ahead. It was during these moments that I would softly hum to myself, a gentle reminder that time was, without a doubt, on my side.

If you find yourself wearing a smile at this very moment, I want you to know that this state of contentment can also be yours. I invite you to take a moment, close your eyes, and envision a life where the blaring alarm clock is no longer necessary to kickstart your day. Imagine waking up to dedicating your time to pursuing the deepest desires of your heart.

Now, as you open your eyes, consider the steps needed to turn this vision into reality. You've officially have taken the first steps to watering your inner seeds.

There has been quite a bit of self-reflection during my journey. Reclaiming my time and owning my day was a pivotal factor for me to leap full-time onto my entrepreneurial desk. My first 90 –days, I found myself working from sunup to sundown, but still asking myself: *"What am I doing with my day?"*

I knew it was time for me to keep better track of my day. The first thing I incorporated on my journey was creating a daily planning practice. Having a firm grasp on your daily activities is vital to the success of any business, especially your own. At the end of my day, I was able to look back at where all my time went, and see if I was allocating it effectively.

Being a wise steward of my time had me finding myself in isolation with my thoughts and making sure I was on track.

When you have a goal, and only you can see the vision for your future you have to protect it at all costs. This is why I stress the importance of staying focused throughout the pages of my journey.

I didn't get staying on track correct all of the time, because I am far from being perfect, doing everything on the straight and narrow path. Like the saying goes, all work and no play— let's just say I had to regain focus on my journey, which is why this book is a guiding source to give you the tools to make your journey less taxing if possible.

When I did find myself wanting to socialize and venture away from my desk to simply share space and time with my family and friends, I took the liberty to do so. Whether it was in person, or just a video call to have a conversation, I quickly discovered that when you are on a path of self-discovery, old conversations tend to not hold as much value as they once did. There are many reasons why people come and go in our lives, and life has a funny way of showing us this. The saying rings true: there is a reason, season or a lifetime timeframe for everyone, you just have to find out what role people play in your life and you in theirs.

I found myself gravitating toward circles and conversations that uplifted, encouraged, and fueled my aspirations which I valued deeply. However, I also came to acknowledge the significance of disentangling from circles that drained my energy and did not provide any impactful punches for my growth. When I found myself in these circles, I politely exited stage left, which was a necessary step I had to identify and take towards preserving my space and time. When you find yourself in circles that are taking up your time, quickly ask yourself what the end goal is, and you will see how fast you end the conversation.

As the days turned from weeks to months, it became evident that the power of intention lay in the choices I made daily. The direction of my success would be dictated by every decision – where, why, and how I chose to spend each second, minute, and hour. During my first 90-days, family and acquaintance circles were no longer innocent, because time taken away from my daily focus could not be replaced. The spotlight was now on me as to how successfully I would manage my time.

I developed a structured day — daily planner blueprint that guided me through the hours. It was about discerning the balance between rest, productivity, and personal engagement. Every day was a puzzle, and every moment contributed to the bigger picture. To apply time effectively, I needed to understand its division— when to rest, when to strive, and when to applaud myself for my personal accomplishments.

The allure of busyness often masks true productivity. It was essential for me to distinguish between the two, to discern whether my actions propelled me forward or trapped me in a cycle of motion without momentum. Each task demanded my attention, and required me to scrutinize it, determining what its purpose was in moving me forward. Without taking the time to ask this question, I risked becoming a hamster on a wheel, exerting and expending energy, but making little progress. Since time was of the essence, I didn't have time to waste.

I made an agreement with myself to stay focused, and with every choice I made, it was an act of self-love and respect for me. It was a commitment to my dreams, a declaration that I and I only held myself responsible for my growth.

My journey was influenced by my decisions, the heavy lifting of productivity, and by marching to the beat of my own drums. I felt this part of life was my best work, a masterpiece in progress, each day adding seeds to my garden and laboring for its full bloom.

I felt the importance of each day as I woke, consciously marking it with urgency, fueling my every move with purpose. Take time to create a structured day that aligns with your aspirations. Be discerning about the circles you move in, and prioritize those things that uplift and support you.

As I encourage you to move along on your journey, it is obvious that the will to succeed rests within your grasp. I realized that I had to be my own timekeeper, and when you embrace your peace and most precious commodity of time, you will see it is ticking in your favor as well.

I found myself utilizing a planner, similar to these shared pages, and now you can take advantage of on your journey. When I felt busy vs. productive, I spent time reviewing where all my time went and was able to pinpoint my time spent down to the seconds.

SCAN QR CODE – Daily Planner Worksheet

Chapter Six

BLOOM IN VULNERABILITY

In this exciting phase of self-transformation and personal growth, it comes as no surprise to me that I found myself digging deep into the examination of my learning habits. I have a natural instinct to seek out knowledge and stay abreast of the ever-evolving times, whether that entails topics like artificial intelligence (AI), digital currency, or the meta universe. We are constantly being exposed to new information and possibilities. Just thinking about the future of photography has me thinking about innovative ideas to incorporate into my company.

In this dynamic and ever-changing journey of life that we are all on together, it is of utmost importance to keep knowledge as a close and trusted companion. Knowledge equips us to navigate the challenges and opportunities that come our way, helping us to adapt and thrive in this ever-evolving world.

When contemplating the *"when, where, and how"* of education, I embrace every facet of it. Whether I'm seated in a conventional, structured university classroom, eagerly soaking up the knowledge shared by an experienced instructor, or taking advantage of budget-friendly approaches, such as Udemy, MasterClass and Teachable, which offers a variety of valuable digital content. In addition to YouTube, which I like to call the goldmine for how-to tutorials and shared knowledge by relatable professionals and creatives. You might also just find yourself in a more laid-back and informal setting, like a jazz infused cigar lounge, amongst friends, indulging in the rich flavors of a captivating glass of *Indelible wine*, created by the R&B legend Adina Howard.

Knowledge often emerges unexpectedly, but that's the beauty regarding learning new information. The *"aha moment"* can happen suddenly, and when it does, you can be confident that I'll be fully engaged and prepare to soak up every bit of shared wisdom. It's as if the universe aligns to deliver the perfect message at just the right moment, and I'm here – arms, head, and heart wide open to embrace it all.

As an artist in photography, I find myself moving towards unconventional learnings that offer a variety of instructors, extensive subject matters and budget friendly prices for my account. I also take time to attend networking opportunities and annual conferences, such as the Wedding and Portraits Photography Intl. (WPPI) conference in my residing city of Las Vegas, which I've attended consistently for five years. When you find your community of like minds and mutual interest, I find it a must for me to embrace and accept the learnings that cultivate my growth.

Self-development occurs both internally and externally, so when I found myself gravitating towards self-mastery, self-empowerment and self-love books, I felt I was aligning with my purpose. I also found myself engaging in discussions surrounding spiritual development and growth that truly resonated with me as I took this journey. You know you've stumbled upon a gem of a book when you catch yourself scribbling notes in the margin or highlighting entire paragraphs as you read. These little treasures I refer to as "love, nuggets," these are nuggets of wisdom, and advice sprinkled throughout the book. They are the kind of insights you can put into action immediately, or they make you nod in fierce agreement, signaling that you've got yourself a truly exceptional book.

When you have a good book, you find yourself asking the critical question, *"am I doing enough to move the needle forward?"* This is something I'll do frequently in my pursuit of meaningful progress. This question often led me down a path of deep self-reflection, where I'd scrutinize my journey. It's those instances of self-doubt or the unease of the unknown that can really mess with your inner peace.

During those moments, I'd often find myself sitting down, silencing the mental chaos and pushing aside the doubts to remind myself that I am indeed doing enough for myself right now, and I'm content with the progress I've made.

Whenever these questions arise within me, they immediately nudge me towards further self-improvement. I start by pinpointing areas where I can actively take corrective measures, focusing on self-healing to understand why I might feel stuck in my progress. I turn the spotlight inward to shine the light on my vulnerabilities that, once exposed, can be strengthened with care, patience, and self-love.

1. *Am I moving too slowly?*

2. *Do my goals need a reevaluation?*

3. *Am I managing my daily schedule effectively?*

Have you heard the saying *"Be kind to yourself?"* This phrase holds a special place in my heart, because when we scrutinize our own shortcomings on our journey, we tend to be harder on ourselves than we would be with others on the same journey. After taking some time to examine this phrase, I was able to identify it comes down to self-expectations. I hold myself to a higher accountability standard than others, meaning if others have shortcomings, there is not a direct effect on you because the outcome falls on them. However, when you identify your *"lack,"* it has to be addressed, and it can be embarrassing when others are holding you accountable and inquiring regarding the when, where and why?

At this very moment, we quickly extend grace to others, but will hesitate or not extend the same to ourselves. I recognize the tendency within myself, and I've made a conscious effort to grant myself the grace and patience that I truly deserve. After all, taking this journey, stepping out from corporate America to follow my passion, is a path that not many choose for themselves, and it's far from easy.

This type of self-introspection tends to rise up within us when we expose ourselves to unfamiliar territories of information. Don't hesitate to select a good book for yourself, whether you decide to explore the aisles of your local library, or a favorite bookstore. Also consider an Audible download if you like to multitask and gain knowledge at the same time, like me.

There are so many amazing books that are out, that hold a wealth of knowledge. Books are blueprints to success, and the title list is based on recommendation, or I have personally read and found value in them. Books are goldmines and once unlocked the knowledge cannot be taken away.

Atomic Habits by James Clear – A compass for constructing positive habits that enact life-altering transformations.

Becoming by Michelle Obama – A memoir of immense power that kindles the flame of embracing one's journey.

The Power of Now by Eckhart Tolle – A guide to inhabiting the present moment, unearthing the treasures of inner tranquility.

Thinking, Fast and Slow by Daniel Kahneman – Brace yourself for a mind-bending exploration of the intricacies of human thought.

The Subtle Art of Not Giving a F*ck by Mark Manson – A candid, no-nonsense roadmap to personal growth and living life to its fullest.

SCAN QR CODE – A Comprehensive book list

Chapter Seven

UPROOTING FEAR

"Don't stop, don't quit." These words were echoing in my mind, my personal mantra, a reassuring decree when doubt and uncertainty cast their shadows. Being firmly aware of my *"why"* served as a powerful motivator for taking my leap. I also had to confront a simple but yet profound question: *"Why not me?"* For the past three years, I'd wanted to become my own boss full time for my photography company. However, when the pandemic swept us up onto an emotional rollercoaster, it brought with it reservations, apprehensions, and, to put it plainly, fear. Yes, it was fear that had been obstructing my blessings all along.

Yes, fear had a grip on me. I had genuine concerns about whether my photography company was the storm during those uncertain times. Moreover, photographers were deemed non-essential workers, and I didn't want to test that categorization. When the world went into lockdown, I retreated to my corporate job to stay put. I took some time to explore the possibilities of growing internally with the company and becoming licensed, but when that Avenue didn't materialize as I hoped, I found myself at a crossroads, unsure about which path to take.

So, another three years passed, while I remained tethered to my corporate desk, working for a company that didn't align with my aspirations or desires. I realize I wasn't quite mentally prepared back then, but I can confidently say that I am more than ready now to step out of my comfort zone, and do what it takes to not only survive, but thrive in my photography business.

If you're curious about the shift that occurred over those three transformational years that compelled me to take action, let me be candid – it all came down to a shift in the conversation within my own mind. I had to summon the courage to push fear aside, and put in the hard work. I firmly believe that, without risk, there are no rewards. If I wanted to demonstrate my commitment to my own company, I needed to step into the unknown. Otherwise, that nagging question would forever follow me *"What if I had taken the chance to believe in myself? Where would I be now?"*

I'm glad to say that I've embraced the gamble, leaving all doubt in fear in the past. I've wholeheartedly committed to moving forward on my path, and fulfilling my purpose.

Fear is a genuine constraint, and if you're grappling with your own fears, I can provide guidance on overcoming the obstacles presented by *"false evidence appearing real."* I can show you how your vision can become a source of blessings in your own future, when you're willing to put in the effort and adequately prepare for the leap.

For quite a few years, I've made mantras and affirmations a part of my daily morning routine. It's a way to get ready for the day, establish a positive vibe, and set my intentions, which has gradually transformed the dialogue within my mind.

When I find myself out of balance, I take time to focus on my chakras which is a Sanskrit word meaning *"wheel"* or *"disk."* A commonly accepted definition for the word chakra is a wheel of energy in your body. These wheels of energy are not something you can physically see, but rather you experience it through feelings, sensations, and your own inner knowing.

When I have a sense of fear creeping up, I remind myself that this energy attachment does not belong here and actively practice releasing attachments until the fear is released through affirmation, and the power of prayer. Affirmations are short phrases you can repeat to change the way you think and feel about yourself.

Here are 7 Chakra affirmations – I have incorporated during my journey that might assist you on yours.

7 CHAKRA AFFIRMATIONS

(I AM) – **MULADHARA** *(THE ROOT CHAKRA)* I am rooted in love and acceptance, and I trust the flow of life to guide me towards my highest good.

(I FEEL) – **SVADHISTHANA** *(THE SACRAL CHAKRA)* I feel confident in my personal power and ability to manifest my desires.

(I DO) – **MANIPURA** *(THE NAVEL CHAKRA)* I attract worthy of love, respect, and success, and I allow myself to receive all that the universe has to offer.

I LOVE) – **ANAHATA** *(THE HEART CHAKRA)* I am surrounded by loving and supportive people who uplift and inspire me.

(I SPEAK) – **VISHUDDHA** *(THE THROAT CHAKRA)* I speak with confidence and assertiveness, while respecting the perspectives of others.

(I SEE) – AJNA *(THE THIRD-EYE CHAKRA)* My intuition is a powerful tool that helps me navigate through life with grace and ease.

(I UNDERSTAND) – SAHASRARA *(THE CROWN CHAKRA)* I understand how to attract and connect to a limitless source of creativity, abundance, health, happiness, and love.

Chapter Eight

GROWING IN SUPPORTIVE SOIL

There are many ways a mentor and mentee relationship connection can start, whether they are word of mouth from a mutual friend, networking events, or like mine, with a thought-provoking social media ad. This ad had all the bells and whistles that got my attention and had me rollover in my bed to get my credit card. I ended up signing up for a masterclass that cost me less than a hundred dollars, but the value I received was priceless.

Without having a call to action in my own head, the voice would not have been received in my heart, and I knew I was ready to receive help and be guided along on my journey and not just by my own efforts.

Every now and then, I have to look around me, and thank God for my life's path that I am on. It's definitely not for the faint of heart, because I've been through my fair share of disappointments, heartbreaks, and tests in my personal and professional walk. I wouldn't change anything about my life because it has made me a stronger woman today, and I am here sharing this one message to inspire you reading my words – that if I can do it, you can too.

When you dive into your leap, I feel you're just waiting for your opportunity to grab ahold of everything that belongs to you.

- TAKING BACK YOUR TIME.

- ENJOYING YOUR CHERISHED RELATIONSHIPS.

- SIMPLY PUT SHATTERING THAT DAMN GLASS CEILING – CREATED TO DISCOURAGE PERSONAL GROWTH.

I want you to hold on tight to my words in life book, and really follow your heart by taking advantage of the information I am sharing with you. If I can help prevent you from making similar mistakes on your journey, I will be that additional voice in your head encouraging you along every step of the way.

I couldn't have picked a more perfect time for my mentor to arrive, because I was open and ready to receive information from a source other than myself. I believe this statement is true:

"When the student is ready, the master will appear." I had to recognize my season of change, finding guidance and support through mentorship. This partnership has been an integral part of my growth and evolution, an alliance that has guided my path as I type down these words.

As you begin to take your own transformative 90-day journey towards passion and purpose, I'd like to share with you the invaluable insights I've gathered in finding my mentor and how you can incorporate this list as well to find your perfect mentor if you ware wanting that extra help on your journey.

These are the top ten guiding principles to consider how a mentor can assist you on your path. They will not only be here to elevate your journey but also ignite your potential:

TOP TEN GUIDING PRINCIPLES

1. **Resonates**: Seek out a mentor whose values and aspirations resonate with your own goals. The alignment of your goals and visions will serve as the foundation for a fruitful mentorship.

2. **Availability**: Your mentor should be accessible and invested in your growth. Their availability to offer guidance, share wisdom, and provide encouragement is pivotal to your journey's success.

3. **Motivation**: The ideal mentor will be an individual who inspires and uplifts you. Their genuine interest in your progress will motivate you to overcome challenges and reach greater heights.

4. **Type of Coach**: Define the specific area in which you require guidance—whether it's spiritual, mental, physical, or financial. Seek a mentor whose expertise aligns with your needs.

5. **Time Commitment**: Assess the time commitment required for effective mentoring. Select a mentor who can dedicate the necessary time to support your growth journey.

6. **Dedication**: Your commitment to the mentorship process is essential. Show your willingness to invest effort, dedication, and intention into making the most of this transformative experience.

7. **Accountability**: Choose a mentor who can hold you accountable for your actions and progress. Their role as an accountability partner will ensure you stay on track towards your goals.

8. **Finances**: Consider the financial aspect of mentorship. Ensure that the mentor's fees align with your budget. If financial constraints arise, explore

options for securing their guidance through creative solutions.

9. **Alignment**: The mentor should comprehend and resonate with your vision. Whether your interactions occur in person or virtually, a deep understanding of your journey is essential.

10. **Compatibility**: Establish a personal connection with your mentor. If you sense a lack of fulfillment or compatibility, don't hesitate to explore alternative mentorship options that better suit your needs.

As you read through the list, I want you to rate each item on a scale of 1 -10, with 1 being the least and 10 being the highest, deciding quality you would want for your mentor, and write down why you are rating with greater or a lesser importance. Once you complete this exercise, I want you to take the top 5, and select only 1 quality that is a dealbreaker, if your mentor doesn't display or offers what you want in a mentor. Lastly, I want you to ask yourself *"am I displaying this same quality for myself?"*

When you find yourself distracted, tired and unmotivated, you have to accept that your mentor is *"the guide and not the ride"* as my mentor has reminded us on numerous occasions. I have to be accountable for my own actions, and look at the woman in the mirror and ask, am I showing up for myself? I had to stay true to my vision of generating multiple streams and rivers of income, growing my photography business clientele and taking on tasks such as going live, holding masterclasses and workshops, checking in with my accountability partners and lastly, being present to win on group calls. When you are consistent in your actions, your vision becomes clear.

It's a divine partnership when you find someone who believes in your potential, and takes time to genuinely share their concerns, and wisdom of strength and encouragement. As I grow and learn on my quest for the financial freedom I desire, I want you along for the ride to witness from beginning to end how I'm laying out the blueprints to a promising future that is within your grasp. So be unafraid to seek guidance from a mentor who can empower you to achieve your goals and aspirations. The risk of taking no action is the costliest risk you can take; all you have to do is start with your inner yes and start moving.

Finding the right mentor can be challenging and a transformative experience altogether. It's not just about identifying someone with expertise; it's about connecting with a person who sees your potential and believes in your ability to bring your aspirations to life. In the same breath, it's also about recognizing your own worth and acknowledging that you deserve a mentor who resonates with your journey.

As you progress along, remember that mentorship is not just a one-way street. In order for you to see growth, you must dedicate your time and commit your invested interest to the process. Hard work and your commitment are equally essential to the equation. Embrace the journey with an open heart and mind. If you are ready to say yes again, and need the tools to get started with me as your mentor, scan your free gift today on page 1, and we can start the journey together.

SCAN QR CODE – Mentor Checklist Worksheet

Chapter Nine

FERTILIZING POSITIVITY

Has anyone ever invited you to join them at sunrise? If not, consider this your invitation to join me for a sunrise broadcast. The golden hour, that magical time within the first hour after sunrise has become my absolute favorite part of the day.

It might surprise some that for over eight years, I've been rising early three to four days out of the week, whether it's to host a morning guided meditation broadcast as LadySunshineLV, or simply to stand on my balcony in awe of the new day. This ritual allows me to greet the day before the sun bathes the Las Vegas desert floor in its warm glow.

Las Vegas has been my home for more than 28 years, and I've witnessed the city change and evolve. However, one thing that remains constant is my deep love for those breathtaking sunrise views.

Imagine seeing the sun first peeking over the mountain tops, as it bathes the world in a brilliant display of fluorescent oranges and vibrant yellows. Its radiant rays, so intense, instantly begin to warm your very soul. This is my reality, and every time, at this very moment, I briefly close my eyes, take a moment to quietly express my gratitude to God for the gift of a new day.

When I reopen my eyes, a smile naturally graces my lips, and my heart swells with an overwhelming sense of calm in appreciation, peace, love, and pure happiness. It's as if I'm witnessing a miracle each time the sun rises to greet me.

During this precious time, I take slow, deep breaths, filling my lungs with positive energy, and exhale slowly, consciously releasing any energies, known or unknown, that may have attached themselves to me. I repeat this practice two to three times, each cycle of deep inhales and exhales serving as a cleansing ritual.

As I continue this mindful breathing, I begin to recite morning affirmations that resonate deeply with my soul. These affirmations marked the beginning of my beautifully divinely guided new day, setting a positive and empowering tone for all that lies ahead.

I intentionally start my day by dedicating time to ground, center, and balance myself because during this time, I feel an incredibly strong connection to God, and sense the loving presence all around me. It's in these moments that I am most attuned to the energy of spirit that surrounds me.

I want to make it clear that I'm not trying to impose my beliefs on anyone, but I feel compelled to acknowledge that my personal journey wouldn't have been possible without the presence of God. If you're reading this book, it's evident that I lead my life with a deep respect and connection to God, and I feel incredibly blessed beyond measures that I am able to experience the Divine's presence.

I'm very aware that I'm guided by a higher power, one that humanity continues to question. Some may refer to this power as source energy, the universe, a spiritual connection, a higher power, or simply God. I use the terms interchangeably because they all represent the source of my profound spiritual connection from within.

There are numerous ways to describe spiritual connection that one experiences when feeling deeply rooted and spiritually connected. I personally believe this connection is a divine presence from the spiritual realm that defies conventional explanation; it's a connection to a higher power. I want to clarify that I'm not a theologian, and I hold no judgment towards your personal beliefs or practices. The fact that our paths have brought us together fills me with gratitude. It enables us to connect on a deep level, continuing on the path of greater enlightenment, personal growth, and the pursuit of our soul's purpose on this journey.

I actively practice the art of the Law of Attraction, a concept that centers around the idea that our thoughts and beliefs can shape our reality. It involves the process of bringing into existence the things we desire by focusing on them positively, maintaining unwavering belief, and aligning our actions with our intentions. This principle suggests that our thoughts and energies act like magnets, attracting experiences and outcomes that resonate with what we consistently think about and visualize.

It's worth noting that I've personally manifested my own journey by regularly affirming my desires to a God and maintaining a *"can do"* belief in myself. I encourage you to explore the power of the Law of Attraction by speaking into existence the things you wholeheartedly desire, while staying unwavering in your thoughts and actions.

I've incorporated meaningful affirmations along my journey that have been extremely powerful for positivity, enlightenment, and growth, which have initiated the shift in my

FERTILIZING POSITIVITY

mindset. It's a simple phrase – *"Everything is always working out for me."* By using this affirmation, and then specifying what aspects of life are indeed working out – such as time, confidence, self-acceptance, or being an uplifter – you can control the transformative power of your thoughts and self-talk.

These carefully chosen words have the remarkable ability to redirect your mindset and alter how you interpret the internal message in your mind. I wholeheartedly encourage you to consider starting a morning routine that includes the practice of affirmations. You'll be amazed at how this simple yet powerful tool can transform your life in a meaningful way.

As a Reiki practitioner, it's imperative for me to establish healthy boundaries with both my inner and outer circles. Engaging in energy work is a combination of rewarding and taxing on the body both physically and mentally. Each morning during my guided meditation broadcast, my viewers join me in my energy space, where I initiate the chakra healing process. I'm fully aware of the significance of my platform, and only a select few viewers have had the opportunity to connect with me after the broadcast concludes. It's essential for all of us to understand that we're human beings with a wide range of emotions, and no one lives in a constant state of positivity. If these words come as a shock to you, let me emphasize that we all share in the human experience, with all its ups and downs. When I find myself being triggered by interactions, I also take a step back, reflect, and make the effort to ground, center, and balance my own emotions.

During my personal journey, I've picked up various techniques and approaches that have been a game changer in handling tough situations. I'm no expert, and I'm still working on the whole, "slow to speak quick to listen" thing, but I've learned that mastering the skill can shift the focus from who's talking to what's being said. So, if you ever find yourself in a situation where your body temperature is starting to bubble up and you're about to get off course, I'd like to share some practices I comingled into my daily routine. These might come in handy when you feel like you've exhausted the positivity overflow.

- **Breathe:** Take a 3 to 4 deep breaths in and release slowly. On the exhale, set your intentions to let go of emotions attached to your disposition.

- **Silence:** Try to release all attachments to the emotions and use silence, because as the saying goes, "silence is golden."

- **Leave:** Remove yourself from the surrounding environment that is drawing you into a negative space.

- **Tap it out**: Use emotional Freedom Techniques, (EFT) or "tapping therapy." This is a form of meditation and stress relief, where you tap specific points on your body, accompanied by positive affirmations or statements. Tapping can be done at your eyebrow point, side of the eye, or even on the chin, to name a few.

There are times where you will have to handle difficult conversations head on, and when that happens, there are many approaches that can be taken to resolve some inevitable interaction. I personally have taken each listed approach listed below – whether professionally or personally, I can relate to each one. Take time to review the list and determine which approach best describes how you've handled difficult conversation in the past, or how you will handle them in the future if presented.

7 APPROACHES FOR DIFFICULT INTERACTIONS

Storytelling: Begin the conversation by sharing a relevant personal or fictional story that relates to the issue at hand. This can help create a relatable context and open the door for a more empathetic and constructive discussion.

Role Reversal: Encourage the other person to express their thoughts and concerns by temporarily switching roles. Let them articulate your perspective, and then you can do the same for them. This approach can foster empathy and mutual understanding.

Visual Aid: Use visual aids, such as diagrams, charts, or illustrations, to illustrate complex points or data during the conversation. Visuals can simplify explanations and make it easier for both parties to grasp the topic.

Third-Party Facilitator: Enlist the help of a neutral third party, such as a mediator or counselor, to facilitate the conversation. They can guide the discussion, ensure fairness, and help find common ground.

Silence: Embrace silence as a tool during the conversation. Allow pauses after statements to give both parties time to reflect and gather their thoughts. Silence can be powerful in prompting deeper reflection and understanding.

Agreement-First: Start the conversation by seeking areas of agreement or common goals. Emphasize shared values and objectives before addressing differences. This approach builds a positive foundation for addressing challenges.

Role Play: Act out different scenarios related to the issue. You and the other person can take on different roles to explore various perspectives and potential outcomes. Role-playing can help identify solutions and unintended consequences.

When you truly grasp these techniques and approaches, your mind is undergoing a transformational shift, and your emotional intelligence is taking control, instead of you trying to steer it.

Chapter Ten

JUST BE PATIENT

Although the first 90 days flew by quickly, I remember the strides I made on this first leg of my journey, just by saying *"yes"* to myself. Deciding to take the leap and bet on my future was rewarding in itself. During this time, I've come to recognize, I put a lot of emphasis on quantifying my progress with numbers, but here's the reality, my initial jump was not about the numbers. It has been about my personal growth, empowerment, fulfillment, and my awakening of self-discovery, self-discipline, and overall transformation. My financial goals, reaching my billionaire status, wasn't going to happen overnight, but I have voiced my desires into the universe, and I'm actively taking steps forward.

The leap I took in April 2023, proved to me that I had the power to decide my own fate. Regardless of what direction I chose, I knew my destiny was contingent on my drive, aspirations, and dedication to my journey and moving forward. Photography has always been my first love, whether my works of art were seen across television screens, or out of sight and only admired by myself. I've been asked the question: when did I turn photography from a hobby into a serious business?

I must admit, I never thought of photography as a hobby. I went from being a student straight into my passion work and immediately had the respect and confidence of others who relied on me to bring their vision to life. The OJT (ON-THE-JOB-TRAINING) propelled me forward, and I believe I had the willpower to keep moving and growing, and how far I wanted to succeed was going to be left up to me.

The key steps I discussed at the beginning of my journey included mindset, setting goals and taking action, which was the product of my leap. My seed of faith was able to be nurtured by the constant reminder that no matter what I did, I could not fail. Why? Because whatever you decide to do, you're fulfilling your purpose. I believe purpose is a combination of who you are, and what you do as a vessel for God. When you are able to share your gifts that were blessed to you by God, this is a form of service; and some reading my words will understand these acts are a way of fulfilling your earthly contract.

When you decide to bet on yourself, your transformation begins to shift to the winning mindset that is always talked about. Not too many people are ready to leave the comforts of their corporate seat, and there is nothing wrong with having reservations on your journey. I want you to know again, my 90 days was a product of a culmination of people saying NO and YES over my lifetime. I had to go through trial and error in my personal and professional life experiences.

Have you ever heard anyone say, *"all you need to have is a mustard seed of faith?"* This is a biblical reference, found in (*Matthew 17:20*) which is a metaphor emphasizing that even a tiny amount of genuine faith can lead to remarkable outcomes or miracles. My desire for financial freedom came to life when I left my job in 2008. When I parted ways, walking across the parking lot to my vehicle, I distinctly recall thinking, 'Now what?' Although these words echoed with fear at that time, I was determined I was not going to allow myself to sulk for long before moving forward.

Before securing new employment, I decided to take some long overdue time off, even if it wasn't my initial plan. During this time, I was able to reignite my passion for photography, by bartering with a local magazine company, traveling around the world with my sister, and attending networking events that turned into photography opportunities. My so-called escape from corporate America lasted for roughly two years. My return back to an office setting was not because I didn't love what I was doing, it was because I wasn't prepared for a life, I didn't yet realize I desired in my twenties. This fearlessness I needed then would not come around for another 13 years, when I would challenge my livelihood and 6 AM - 2 PM schedule.

I believe my steps are divinely guided by God, and I have been able to put myself in a position to hear directly that it was my time. If you're shaking in your shoes at the thought of taking the first step, and saying it's my time — If this is you, let me encourage you that just by saying yes, you have taken the biggest first step of them all. This is the step of faith, your start of a new beginning.

Chapter Eleven

I WANT MY FLOWERS

*A*RMS OUTSTRETCHED WITH HEAD HELD HIGH, LEANING BACK, AND ALLOWING THE SUNLIGHT TO WARM MY FACE "I DID IT!" ALLOWING GRATITUDE TO WASH OVER ME, WITH A SIMPLE SIGH ESCAPING MY LIPS, I WAS IN PURE BLISS. JUST TAKING IT ALL IN TO SAY TO MYSELF "GOD IS GOOD."

I know my journey is far from being over, but I can see my path clearly and the seeds that were sown are now budding all around me. When you are ready to get your hands dirty, and really uproot the fear of inactivity and lack of productivity, that is when you will know a brighter tomorrow is possible while living for today.

Here's to not stopping or quitting, and embracing the beautiful journey of self-discovery, success, and fulfillment. Are you ready to take this path with courage, determination, and a firm belief that you now embody everything you need to be successful? I know I am ready to achieve greatness and create a life that is rich in the ease of receiving my abundance. My mind, body and soul are ready for the blessings of everything – I have spoken and unspoken to be ushered into my life with open arms.

These three months have been nothing short of transformative, and I can proudly say that I have not just survived, but my very existence has been transformed with the power of my own "*YES!*" I've had the unwavering support of my entire family and circle of friends during my discovery period, and being cheered on as I was able to find my footing.

Despite the emotional ups and downs on my journey, I've persevered. My ultimate goal was to keep moving forward and progressing, and I refused to give up on myself. I believe my journey can service as a blueprint for someone's fresh start, and perhaps that someone is you. This path isn't for everyone and I had to look in the mirror and ask myself "when will I bet on myself? If you're now asking yourself the same questions, you're nurturing the seeds of change within, and the answer will reveal itself on due time.

In these 90 days, I reclaimed my time, my power, and my energy unapologetically choosing myself on this journey. Each morning I awoke with the realization that it was a really good day to be me. Get ready for my upcoming book, "365 Days of a New Way of Life." within these pages, you'll witness a fresh attitude, conquer self-limiting beliefs, and redefinition of who I am.

There's no better time than the present to reintroduce myself, as a better, stronger and version of me. With my footsteps firmly planted in the soil of my own potential, you'll see how my life was reshaped in these "365 Days of a New Way of Life.' I may not know what tomorrow brings, but in my todays, I'm infusing my life with positivity, prosperity, and my goal of generating multiple streams of income, The possibilities are limitless.

I want to personally thank you for taking the time to explore the pages of *"Full Bloom."* Now, you've become a part of my journey. If my words have ignited a spark in you to start pursuing your next level, I invite you to join me.

Simply scan your free gift and signup today for your next level. You hold the seeds of change in your hands, you don't have to walk this journey alone. Accept my open invitation, take action for your better tomorrow, that begins with a single step – the power of saying, *YES*!

SUPPORT THE AUTHOR

REVIEW FULL BLOOM ON AMAZON!

Journal

"History has shown us that courage can be contagious, and hope can take on a life of its own."

Michelle Obama

"Change will not come if we wait for some other person or some other time. We are the ones we've been waiting for. We are the change that we seek."

Barack Obama

"There is no such thing as failure. Failure is just life trying to move us in another direction."

Oprah Winfrey

"Be passionate and move forward with gusto every single hour of every single day until you reach your goal."

Ava Duvernay

"I LEARNED EARLY ON THE MAGIC OF LIFE IS HAVING A VISION, HAVING FAITH AND THEN GOING FOR IT."

ELAINE WELTEROTH

"I AM LUCKY THAT WHATEVER FEAR I HAVE INSIDE ME, MY DESIRE TO WIN IS ALWAYS STRONGER."

SERENA WILLIAMS

"Success is to be measured not so much by the position that one has reached in life as by the obstacles which he has overcome while trying to succeed."

Booker T. Washington

"If you wait for the perfect time,

you will always be waiting."

Adina Howard

"There are two rules in life: Number 1, never quit! Number 2, never forget rule number one."

Duke Ellington

"Don't sit down and wait for the opportunities to come. Get up and make them."

Madam C.J. Walker

"I'M NO LONGER ACCEPTING THE THINGS I CANNOT CHANGE...I'M CHANGING THE THINGS I CANNOT ACCEPT."

ANGELA DAVIS

> "IF THEY DON'T GIVE YOU A SEAT AT THE TABLE,
>
> MAKE YOUR OWN."
>
> Tyler Perry

ACKNOWLEDGEMENT

I never imagined I'd be in this position, expressing my gratitude for my journey in a book, but here I am. Life has a way of leading us down unexpected paths, often ones we only dreamt of. Now, I can officially check off "*author*" from my life-list. Writing this book has truly been a transformational journey of growth and fulfillment, with countless soul connections along the way. To my amazing support system, you mean the world to me, and I want to sincerely thank every single person for surrounding me with love and support.

I am also grateful for everyone who have shared kind words, whether directly or indirectly, and supported my various business endeavors, whether big or small.

Thank you. London Howard

REFERENCES

Chained to the desk in a hybrid world (NYU Press, 2023) By Bryan Robinson,

Ph.D. *www.forbes.com*

https://www.forbes.com/sites/bryanrobinson/2022/05/03/

discover-the-top-5-reasons-workers-want-to-quit-their-

jobs/?sh=41ff1add5d46

Consumers Affair

https://www.consumeraffairs.com/finance/financial-plans-amid-the-great-

resignation.html

7 Chakras: Your Guide to The 7

Chakras & Their Meaning *www.yogainternational.com*

https://yogainternational.com/article/view/what-are-the-7-chakras/

Affirmations: What They Are, Health Benefits,

and Getting Started By Rena Goldman

https://www.everydayhealth.com/emotional-health/what-are-affirmations

SOCIAL MEDIA

Let's stay connected by following me on social media.

- instagram.com/conversationwithlondon
- facebook.com/conversationwithlondon
- twitter.com/convowithlondon
- linkedin.com/conversationwithlondon

Made in the USA
Las Vegas, NV
07 November 2023